VIOLET LA CROIX

Capybaras: Nature's Social Giants

Copyright © 2023 by Violet La Croix

All rights reserved. No part of this publication may be reproduced, stored or transmitted in any form or by any means, electronic, mechanical, photocopying, recording, scanning, or otherwise without written permission from the publisher. It is illegal to copy this book, post it to a website, or distribute it by any other means without permission.

First edition

This book was professionally typeset on Reedsy.
Find out more at reedsy.com

Contents

Chapter 1: Introduction to Capybaras — 1
Chapter 2: Capybara Ecology — 6
Chapter 3: Capybara Social Life — 12
Chapter 4: Capybara Behavior and Intelligence — 17
Chapter 5: Capybaras in Human Culture — 22
Chapter 6: Capybara Communication — 27
Chapter 7: Capybaras and their Predators — 33
Chapter 8: Capybaras and Human Agriculture — 38
Chapter 9: Capybaras in Captivity — 44
Chapter 10: Future of Capybaras — 50
Conclusion: Capybaras - Nature's Social Giants — 56

Chapter 1: Introduction to Capybaras

Capybaras, nature's social giants, are fascinating and unique creatures that capture the hearts of both scientists and nature enthusiasts alike. In this chapter, we will explore what capybaras are, their evolutionary history, and their remarkable physical characteristics and adaptations that have enabled them to thrive in diverse environments.

1.1 What are Capybaras?

Capybaras (Hydrochoerus hydrochaeris) are the largest rodents in the world, belonging to the family Caviidae. They are native to South America, primarily found in countries such as Brazil, Venezuela, Colombia, Argentina, and Paraguay. Often referred to as "water pigs" due to their semi-aquatic lifestyle, capybaras are closely related to guinea pigs and rock cavies.

These social animals have a robust and barrel-shaped body, with a blunt face and small ears. They possess short, sturdy legs and partially webbed feet, ideal for swimming and navigating through marshy landscapes. The average adult capybara stands around 2 feet tall at the shoulder and can weigh between 100 to 150 pounds, with some individuals reaching up to 200 pounds.

Capybaras are herbivores, mainly feeding on grasses and aquatic plants. Their unique digestive system allows them to efficiently extract nutrients from their plant-based diet. Being herbivores, capybaras play an essential role in their ecosystems by influencing vegetation growth and shaping the landscape.

1.2 Evolutionary History of Capybaras

The evolutionary history of capybaras is rooted in ancient times. Fossil evidence suggests that their ancestors first appeared around 30 to 40 million years ago during the Oligocene epoch. The earliest capybara-like creatures were relatively small and lived in dense forests.

As South America underwent significant geological changes, such as the formation of the Andes Mountains and the emergence of the Amazon Basin, capybaras adapted to new environments and diversified. Their size increased over time, and they developed specific traits that enabled them to thrive in both terrestrial and aquatic habitats.

The capybara's unique adaptations allowed them to become highly successful herbivores, utilizing both land and water resources. Their semi-aquatic lifestyle not only provided them with ample food sources but also offered safety from terrestrial predators. This adaptability and resilience contributed to their survival and spread throughout South America.

1.3 Physical Characteristics and Adaptations

Capybaras have several physical characteristics and adaptations that make them remarkable creatures well-suited to their environment.

Semi-Aquatic Lifestyle: Capybaras are perfectly adapted for a semi-aquatic lifestyle. Their webbed feet and strong swimming abilities allow them to move effortlessly through water, making it easier to escape predators and access aquatic plants. They are commonly found near rivers, ponds, and marshes.

Thermoregulation: Given their habitat's tropical and subtropical regions, capybaras have developed effective thermoregulation mechanisms. They are known to spend much of their day in water or mud, which helps regulate their body temperature and prevent overheating.

Social Behavior: Capybaras are highly social animals, living in large groups known as "herds" or "groups." These herds can consist of 10 to 40 individuals, promoting cooperation, protection against predators, and communication. Within the group, they establish a hierarchy that determines access to resources and mating opportunities.

Communication: Capybaras communicate using a combination of vocalizations, body language, and scent markings. They have a repertoire of vocalizations, including purring, barking, and whistling, to convey various messages to their group members.

Digestive Adaptations: As herbivores, capybaras possess unique digestive adaptations. They are hindgut fermenters, meaning they have a specialized compartment in their digestive system called the cecum, where bacteria break down fibrous plant materials. This adaptation enables them to efficiently extract nutrients from their fibrous plant-based diet.

Predator Avoidance: Capybaras face threats from predators such as jaguars, caimans, and anacondas. To avoid predation, they rely on their excellent senses of smell and hearing. When a potential threat is detected, capybaras can quickly seek refuge in water, where they are less vulnerable to predators.

1.4 Habitat and Distribution

Capybaras are well-adapted to a variety of habitats across South America, making them one of the most widely distributed mammals on the continent. Their range extends from eastern Panama to northern Argentina and Uruguay. Capybaras can be found in diverse environments, including savannas, grasslands, wetlands, marshes, and tropical rainforests.

The semi-aquatic nature of capybaras makes water bodies a crucial component of their habitat. They prefer regions with access to freshwater sources like rivers, streams, and ponds, where they can swim, cool off, and find abundant food resources. Water serves as both a means of protection from predators and a convenient pathway for travel.

In tropical rainforests, capybaras often inhabit the forest edges or areas with dense vegetation along rivers. They can also be found in more open habitats like savannas and grasslands, where they graze on the available vegetation. These adaptable creatures have successfully established themselves in both rural and urban areas, sometimes even residing near human settlements and agricultural lands.

1.5 Behavior and Social Structure

Capybaras are highly social animals, and their social structure is a key aspect of their lives. They live in large groups known as herds, bands, or groups, typically consisting of 10 to 40 individuals. Within the herd, they establish a hierarchy based on dominance and territorial behavior. The alpha male and female usually hold the highest positions in the group, and they have priority access to resources and mating opportunities.

Social bonding is a fundamental part of capybara behavior. They engage in mutual grooming, vocalizations, and playful activities to strengthen social ties and maintain group cohesion. Such social behavior is crucial for their survival, as it helps protect individuals from predators and provides support during times of stress or danger.

Capybaras are generally docile and non-aggressive towards their group members. However, disputes and conflicts can still occur, especially during mating seasons or when resources are limited. In such situations, dominant individuals may assert their authority, and fights can break out, though they are usually brief and not severe.

As crepuscular animals, capybaras are most active during dawn and dusk, while spending the hottest hours of the day resting or cooling off in water. Their semi-aquatic lifestyle also involves frequent bathing, which helps regulate body temperature and removes parasites from their fur.

1.6 Conservation Status and Threats

Despite being widespread across South America, capybaras face certain conservation challenges due to human activities and habitat changes. As of my knowledge cutoff in September 2021, the International Union for Conservation of Nature (IUCN) listed the capybara as a species of "Least Concern," indicating that the population is relatively stable. However, localized threats and pressures can impact specific populations.

Habitat loss is one of the primary concerns for capybara conservation. Human activities, such as deforestation, agricultural expansion, and urbanization, lead to the destruction and fragmentation of their natural habitats. As their habitats shrink, capybaras are forced to live in smaller and more isolated areas, making them more vulnerable to predation and limiting access to resources.

Poaching and hunting also pose a threat to capybara populations. In some regions, they are hunted for their meat and skin, which is considered a delicacy or used for traditional purposes. Overhunting can deplete local populations and disrupt social structures within herds.

Additionally, human-wildlife conflict arises when capybaras encroach on agricultural lands. They are known to graze on crops, leading to conflicts with farmers and retaliatory actions that can result in harm to capybaras or even their deaths.

Climate change is another potential threat to capybaras. Alterations in temperature and precipitation patterns can affect their habitat and the availability of food and water resources. As capybaras rely heavily on water bodies for their survival, any changes in water availability or quality can have significant impacts on their populations.

Conservation efforts for capybaras involve several strategies, including habitat protection, promoting coexistence with humans, and raising awareness about the importance of these creatures in maintaining ecosystem balance. Research on capybara ecology and behavior is crucial for understanding their needs and developing effective conservation measures.

Chapter 2: Capybara Ecology

Capybaras, as nature's social giants, play a crucial role in their ecosystems. In this chapter, we will delve into their ecology, focusing on their diet and feeding habits, the role they play in ecosystems, and their interactions with other species.

2.1 Capybara Diet and Feeding Habits

Capybaras are herbivores with a strictly vegetarian diet. Their diet primarily consists of various plant materials, including grasses, aquatic plants, fruits, and tree bark. The availability of food resources in their habitats determines their feeding habits and movement patterns.

During the wet season, when their habitats are abundant with fresh vegetation and water sources, capybaras tend to graze extensively. They are particularly fond of grasses, which make up a significant portion of their diet. Their ability to crop grasses efficiently is aided by their sharp incisors, which allow them to cut through tough plant material.

As the dry season approaches and water sources diminish, capybaras may shift their feeding habits. They become more opportunistic, relying on a broader range of plants, including fallen fruits and leaves from trees and shrubs. This adaptability enables them to persist through periods of food scarcity.

Capybaras are also known to practice coprophagy, a behavior in which they consume their own feces. This behavior aids in the digestion of certain plant components, as the cecotropes, or soft feces, are rich in essential nutrients and microbes that assist in breaking down fibrous plant material in their hindgut.

Their herbivorous diet plays a vital role in shaping the landscapes they inhabit. By grazing on grasses and aquatic plants, capybaras influence plant growth and distribution, which can have cascading effects on other species within the ecosystem.

2.2 Role of Capybaras in Ecosystems

Capybaras are considered keystone species in their ecosystems, meaning their presence and activities have a disproportionate impact on the entire community. As herbivores, they significantly influence the structure and composition of vegetation in their habitats.

By grazing on vegetation, capybaras control the growth of grasses and aquatic plants, preventing them from becoming overgrown and choking water bodies. This allows for the maintenance of open spaces, which are essential for various species like birds and reptiles that require unobstructed access to water and nesting sites.

Moreover, their grazing activities promote plant diversity by creating diverse habitats. By selectively feeding on certain plant species, capybaras indirectly foster the growth of other plants, contributing to the overall richness of plant life in their environment.

The semi-aquatic behavior of capybaras also influences aquatic ecosystems. Their presence near water bodies can create pathways and clearings, making it easier for other animals to access water. Additionally, the disturbances caused by their wallowing and bathing activities can create microhabitats for various aquatic organisms.

Furthermore, capybaras contribute to nutrient cycling in their ecosystems. Their coprophagy behavior helps redistribute essential nutrients, such as nitrogen and phosphorus, back into the environment through the recycling of plant material. This nutrient cycling plays a vital role in maintaining soil fertility and supporting the growth of vegetation.

In summary, capybaras are ecosystem engineers that actively shape their habitats through their feeding habits and interactions with vegetation and water bodies. Their influence on plant distribution, nutrient cycling, and habitat creation has far-reaching effects on other species within the ecosystem.

2.3 Interaction with Other Species

Capybaras are social animals that interact not only with their own group members but also with various other species within their ecosystems. Some of the key interactions include:

Predator-Prey Relationships: Capybaras face predation from a range of species, including jaguars, caimans, anacondas, and large birds of prey. Their social structure and vigilance in groups provide some protection against predators. When a threat is detected, capybaras quickly seek refuge in water, which serves as a vital escape route from terrestrial predators.

Commensalism and Mutualism: Capybaras can exhibit commensalistic relationships with other species. For instance, birds like the cattle egret and oxpecker are often seen perched on capybaras, feeding on insects and parasites that are disturbed when the capybaras graze or bathe. The birds benefit from a steady source of food, while the capybaras are relatively unaffected by their presence.

Competitive Interactions: Capybaras may compete with other herbivores for food resources, especially during periods of food scarcity. In some regions, they may encounter competition with livestock for grazing areas, leading to potential conflicts with farmers.

Species Interactions in Water Bodies: The semi-aquatic lifestyle of capybaras brings them into contact with various aquatic species. They often share water bodies with caimans, turtles, and fish. While capybaras are not direct competitors with these species, their activities can have indirect effects on the availability of resources in the water, influencing the behavior and distribution of aquatic organisms.

Influence on Bird Nesting: Capybara groups provide protection to birds nesting on their backs. For example, the yellow-rumped cacique, a bird species, may build its nest on a capybara's back, using the capybara's social structure and vigilance as protection against predators.

Overall, capybaras are integral components of their ecosystems, and their interactions with other species play a vital role in maintaining the balance and health of the surrounding environment.

2.4 Migratory Patterns and Seasonal Behavior

CHAPTER 2: CAPYBARA ECOLOGY

Capybaras exhibit fascinating migratory patterns and seasonal behaviors as they adapt to the changing environmental conditions of their habitats. These movements are influenced by factors such as food availability, water levels, temperature, and the need to find suitable areas for breeding and raising their young.

During the wet season, when rainfall is abundant, many capybara populations experience an increase in water levels in rivers, streams, and ponds. This expansion of aquatic habitats not only provides them with more accessible water sources but also increases the availability of aquatic plants, which are a significant part of their diet. Consequently, capybaras tend to concentrate in wetlands and flooded areas during this period.

As the dry season approaches and water sources begin to recede, capybaras may undergo migratory movements in search of better grazing opportunities and alternative water bodies. They may travel considerable distances to find suitable feeding grounds and escape the threat of predators. These migratory movements often involve group travel, which can be beneficial for social cohesion and safety.

Capybaras are known to be highly adaptive in their migratory behavior. In some areas, they may follow traditional migratory routes that have been established over generations, while in other regions, their movements may be more opportunistic, responding to changing local conditions.

The migratory patterns and seasonal behavior of capybaras are crucial aspects of their ecology, as they impact the distribution of capybara populations and their interactions with other species in the ecosystem.

2.5 Reproduction and Parental Care

Reproduction in capybaras is a significant event in their social structure and group dynamics. Mating typically occurs during the wet season when food resources are plentiful, and water levels are high. Dominant males, often the alpha male in a group, have priority in mating opportunities and access to females in estrus.

The courtship behavior of capybaras involves vocalizations, scent markings, and physical interactions. Males may vocalize and establish their territories by scent marking, while females signal their readiness to mate through specific behaviors and scents.

Gestation in capybaras lasts approximately 150 days, after which the female gives birth to a litter of pups. The average litter size is around three to eight pups, although it can vary depending on environmental conditions and the health of the mother. Newborn capybaras are precocial, meaning they are relatively mature and mobile at birth. They have open eyes, can walk, and can even graze within hours of being born.

Parental care is a shared responsibility among the group members. While the mother is the primary caregiver, other females and even non-breeding males may assist in protecting and caring for the young. This cooperative care helps ensure the survival of the pups, especially during the vulnerable early stages of life.

Capybara young are nursed by their mother for several months, but they also begin to eat solid food early on. As they grow, they become more independent and gradually integrate into the social dynamics of the group.

The social structure of capybaras plays a crucial role in the successful reproduction and upbringing of their young. The cooperative care and protection provided by the group enhance the survival chances of the pups, allowing them to grow and thrive in their natural environment.

2.6 Impact of Environmental Changes on Capybara Populations

Capybara populations are highly susceptible to environmental changes due to their dependence on specific habitat conditions and resources. Human activities and climate change pose significant threats to these social giants and can have detrimental effects on their populations.

Habitat Destruction and Fragmentation: The conversion of natural habitats for agricultural purposes, urban development, and infrastructure projects has resulted in the destruction and fragmentation of capybara habitats. Reduced access to suitable areas for grazing and water sources can lead to population decline and increased vulnerability to predation.

Climate Change: As climate change alters temperature and precipitation patterns, capybara habitats may experience changes in vegetation growth, water availability, and the timing of seasons. These shifts can disrupt the timing of reproductive cycles, migratory patterns, and feeding behaviors, impacting the overall health and stability of capybara populations.

Human-Wildlife Conflict: Capybaras sometimes encounter conflict with humans due to their grazing activities on crops and competition for resources. In some cases, this conflict can lead to retaliation, hunting, or relocation, putting additional pressure on capybara populations.

Disease Transmission: The proximity of capybaras to human settlements and livestock increases the risk of disease transmission between species. Diseases that may not affect capybaras significantly can pose a threat to other vulnerable wildlife or domestic animals, leading to potential ecosystem imbalances.

Hunting and Poaching: Although capybaras are protected in many areas, they are still hunted for their meat and skin in certain regions. Unsustainable hunting can lead to population declines, especially if hunting targets reproductive adults.

Conservation efforts aimed at protecting capybara populations must address these challenges by focusing on habitat preservation, mitigating human-wildlife conflict, and promoting sustainable land use practices. Understanding the ecological needs of capybaras, their interactions with other species, and their role in maintaining ecosystem balance is crucial for implementing effective conservation strategies.

Chapter 3: Capybara Social Life

Capybaras are highly social animals known for their complex and intricate social structures. In this chapter, we will explore the fascinating world of capybara social life, including their complex social structure, family units, hierarchies, and the various forms of communication that play a pivotal role in their interactions with group members.

3.1 Complex Social Structure

Capybaras live in large groups known as herds, bands, or groups. These social structures are characterized by intricate relationships and behaviors that facilitate cooperation, protection, and communication within the group. Herd size can vary but typically ranges from 10 to 40 individuals, though larger groups have been observed in certain areas with ample resources.

The social structure of capybaras is multi-layered, with different levels of social interactions and hierarchies. At the core of the social structure are the alpha male and alpha female, who hold the highest positions in the hierarchy. They are the dominant pair and have priority access to resources, mating opportunities, and prime resting spots.

Beneath the alpha pair, there are other individuals with varying degrees of dominance. These social hierarchies are established and maintained through ritualized behaviors and interactions, such as aggressive displays, vocalizations, and physical contact. Lower-ranking individuals generally yield to higher-ranking ones in matters related to access to food and water or determining group movements.

The social structure of capybaras is not fixed and can change over time due

CHAPTER 3: CAPYBARA SOCIAL LIFE

to various factors such as the arrival of new individuals, the loss of dominant members, or changes in environmental conditions. These changes may lead to shifts in hierarchies and influence the dynamics within the group.

3.2 Family Units and Hierarchies

Within capybara herds, family units form the basis of social organization. Family units are typically composed of a dominant breeding pair (alpha male and female) and their offspring. The alpha female plays a central role in organizing and leading the group. She is the primary caregiver to her young, ensuring their safety and guiding them through their early stages of life.

Other female members of the group also participate in caring for the young, forming a cooperative care system. They may assist the alpha female by protecting and nursing her offspring. This cooperative care enhances the survival chances of the young capybaras and strengthens social bonds within the group.

Male capybaras, especially the alpha male, play a vital role in protecting the group from potential threats. They are vigilant and watchful, scanning their surroundings for predators and other dangers. Their alertness helps to ensure the safety of the entire group.

The family units and hierarchies within capybara herds foster a sense of social cohesion and cooperation. Each member contributes to the group's well-being, making it a formidable force against potential threats and challenges.

3.3 Communication Among Capybaras

Communication is crucial for maintaining social harmony and coordination within capybara herds. Capybaras use a combination of vocalizations, body language, and scent markings to convey various messages to their group members.

Vocalizations: Capybaras produce a wide range of vocalizations to communicate with each other. Common vocalizations include purring, barking, whining, and whistling. Purring is often associated with contentment and relaxation, while barking is used as an alarm call to alert the group to potential dangers.

Body Language: Capybaras use various body postures and movements to express their intentions and emotions. For instance, raising their heads high is a sign of alertness and vigilance, while lowering their heads is a submissive gesture. They also engage in playful behaviors, such as running and jumping, to strengthen social bonds within the group.

Scent Markings: Scent plays a significant role in capybara communication. They have specialized scent glands located near their eyes and on their backs. By rubbing these glands on vegetation and objects, they leave scent markings that convey information about their presence, reproductive status, and territorial boundaries. Scent marking helps reinforce social hierarchies and reduce potential conflicts within the group.

Visual Signals: Capybaras use visual signals, such as ear movements and facial expressions, to communicate non-verbally with other group members. For example, flicking their ears or raising their heads can be used as signals to indicate alertness or submission.

These communication methods facilitate coordination during various activities, such as foraging, grooming, and group movements. Effective communication is essential for capybaras to thrive in their social groups and maintain their unique social structure.

3.4 Play and Social Interactions

Play is an essential aspect of capybara social life and is commonly observed among young individuals within the group. Play behaviors serve multiple purposes, including the development of social skills, strengthening social bonds, and reducing tension within the group. Playful interactions also allow young capybaras to practice essential survival skills in a safe and non-threatening environment.

Playful activities among capybaras can involve chasing, wrestling, running, and engaging in mock fights. These interactions are often accompanied by vocalizations and enthusiastic body language. Play is not limited to capybaras of the same age; individuals of different ages and ranks can also participate, contributing to the group's sense of unity.

Playing also helps establish and reinforce hierarchies within the group. Dominant individuals may engage in gentle play with subordinates, which reinforces the hierarchy while also strengthening social bonds. Play also plays a role in conflict resolution, as it allows capybaras to express their feelings and emotions without escalating conflicts into aggression.

3.5 Bonding and Affection

Capybaras are highly social and form strong bonds within their groups. Bonding and affectionate behaviors are prevalent among family members and close companions. Mutual grooming is a common way for capybaras to demonstrate affection and strengthen social bonds.

During mutual grooming, individuals use their teeth and mouths to clean and groom each other's fur. This behavior not only helps maintain good hygiene within the group but also fosters trust and cooperation. Grooming is particularly important for the social structure of capybaras, as it plays a role in establishing and maintaining hierarchies.

Bonding and affection are especially evident among members of family units. The alpha female, in particular, plays a central role in nurturing and caring for her offspring. Other females in the group also participate in grooming and caring for the young, reinforcing the sense of family and social cohesion.

While grooming is a common form of bonding, other behaviors also indicate affection. Capybaras may rest close to each other, engage in gentle nuzzling, or sleep in contact with one another. These behaviors reinforce social bonds and contribute to the overall stability and harmony of the group.

3.6 Social Conflicts and Resolutions

Like any social species, capybaras experience conflicts and disagreements within their groups. Social conflicts can arise for various reasons, including competition for resources, mating opportunities, or establishing dominance within the hierarchy.

When conflicts occur, capybaras rely on a series of ritualized behaviors to resolve disputes without resorting to aggression. Aggressive interactions are generally avoided, as they can be costly and lead to injuries. Instead, capybaras engage in submissive behaviors, such as lowering their heads, displaying their bellies, or moving away, to defuse tension and avoid escalation.

Capybaras also use vocalizations and body language to communicate their intentions and emotions during conflicts. Clear communication is crucial in preventing misunderstandings and finding resolutions to conflicts. For example, a dominant individual may give a warning vocalization to signal its position and authority, and subordinates respond by acknowledging their lower rank.

Cooperative care within the group also plays a role in resolving conflicts. Lower-ranking individuals may show deference to dominant members, reducing the likelihood of confrontations. Additionally, when conflicts arise, other group members may intervene to separate individuals or mediate the situation, promoting reconciliation and restoring social harmony.

Conflict resolution is crucial for maintaining stable social structures and minimizing disruptions within capybara groups. The ability to resolve conflicts peacefully allows them to maintain their complex social hierarchies and cooperative behaviors, which are essential for survival and success in their environments.

Chapter 4: Capybara Behavior and Intelligence

Capybaras are not only social animals but also demonstrate impressive problem-solving skills, learning abilities, and a level of intelligence that makes them fascinating subjects of study. In this chapter, we will delve into the behavior and intelligence of capybaras, exploring their problem-solving skills, learning capabilities, and the intriguing aspects of tool use and innovation.

4.1 Capybaras' Problem-Solving Skills

Capybaras exhibit problem-solving skills in various situations, adapting to challenges presented by their environment. One of the most remarkable examples of their problem-solving abilities is related to their semi-aquatic lifestyle. When faced with the challenge of escaping from predators on land, capybaras quickly retreat to water bodies, where they are adept swimmers and find safety from terrestrial threats.

Furthermore, capybaras demonstrate problem-solving skills in foraging behavior. As herbivores, they need to find and access vegetation for sustenance. They are skilled grazers and are known to efficiently crop grasses using their sharp incisors. Additionally, they are highly adaptable in their feeding habits, which allows them to switch to alternative food sources during periods of scarcity.

In captive settings, capybaras have been observed solving puzzles and navigating maze-like environments to obtain rewards, showcasing their cognitive abilities. Their problem-solving skills are likely honed through experiences in their natural environment, where they encounter various challenges and learn to adapt to them over time.

4.2 Learning Abilities and Memory

Capybaras exhibit impressive learning abilities and have an excellent memory, allowing them to remember important information about their environment, social dynamics, and food sources. Learning from experiences and interactions with their surroundings is essential for their survival and well-being.

Young capybaras learn social behaviors, communication cues, and survival skills from their family members and group members. They observe and imitate the behaviors of older individuals, helping them integrate into the group and understand their place within the hierarchy.

Memory is also crucial for capybaras' daily activities. They remember the locations of food sources, water bodies, and safe resting spots. Such memory allows them to navigate their environment efficiently and ensures they can access essential resources when needed.

In the context of predation, capybaras remember the alarm calls and signals given by group members when danger is detected. This helps them quickly respond to threats and seek safety in the face of potential danger.

In captivity, capybaras have demonstrated the ability to learn from training sessions and form associations between specific behaviors and rewards. Their capacity to learn and remember information makes them amenable to training and interaction with humans in controlled settings.

4.3 Tool Use and Innovation

Tool use is a behavior often associated with higher intelligence in animals. While capybaras do not exhibit extensive tool use like some other species, they have been observed using objects in innovative ways to facilitate certain behaviors.

One example of tool use in capybaras is their use of sticks or logs as makeshift grooming tools. When grooming hard-to-reach areas on their bodies, they may use their front paws to hold and manipulate a stick or log to access those spots more effectively.

Additionally, capybaras have been observed using vegetation, such as

CHAPTER 4: CAPYBARA BEHAVIOR AND INTELLIGENCE

branches or leaves, to create shelters or nests. These improvised structures provide some protection from the elements and help them conserve body heat during colder periods.

Innovation is also evident in capybaras' feeding behavior. They may explore and experiment with various plant species, even those they are not familiar with, to expand their diet and adapt to changes in food availability.

While the tool use and innovation of capybaras may not be as extensive as some other species, their ability to utilize objects in creative ways showcases their intelligence and adaptability to their environment.

4.4 Emotional Intelligence in Capybaras

Emotional intelligence refers to an individual's ability to recognize, understand, and manage their own emotions and the emotions of others. While it is challenging to measure emotional intelligence directly in animals, studies suggest that capybaras, as highly social and intelligent creatures, possess a degree of emotional intelligence that aids in their social interactions and survival.

Capybaras demonstrate a range of emotional expressions through their body language, vocalizations, and interactions with other group members. They can convey emotions such as contentment, fear, curiosity, and affection through their facial expressions and vocalizations. For instance, their purring vocalizations are often associated with a relaxed and content state, while barking may signal alarm or distress.

As social animals, capybaras rely on emotional cues to maintain social cohesion and harmony within their groups. They respond to the emotional signals of other group members, which helps establish and maintain social bonds and alleviate tension during conflicts.

Capybaras' emotional intelligence is especially evident in their nurturing and cooperative care behaviors. Mothers display strong maternal instincts and affectionate behaviors toward their young, demonstrating their emotional attachment and care. Other group members also engage in grooming and protection of the young, showing empathy and concern for their well-being.

Studies on animal cognition have also explored the concept of empathy in capybaras. Empathy refers to an individual's ability to understand and share the feelings of others. Observations of capybara groups have suggested that when one individual is distressed or alarmed, others in the group respond with increased vigilance and attention, indicating a potential display of empathy.

While emotional intelligence in capybaras remains a topic of ongoing research and exploration, their social behaviors and responses to emotional cues provide valuable insights into their cognitive and emotional capabilities.

4.5 Responses to External Stimuli

Capybaras display a range of responses to external stimuli in their environment. Their reactions are shaped by their social dynamics, survival instincts, and experiences with different environmental factors. Some common responses to external stimuli include:

Alarm Calls: When capybaras detect potential threats, they emit alarm calls, usually in the form of high-pitched barks. These vocalizations alert other group members to the presence of danger and trigger a collective response, such as seeking safety in water or adopting a heightened state of vigilance.

Group Cohesion: Capybaras are highly social animals, and their responses to external stimuli often involve the entire group. When faced with a threat, they rely on their collective strength and numbers to increase their chances of survival. Group members may huddle together, maintain physical contact, and synchronize their movements to stay close and protected.

Flight Response: Capybaras are skilled swimmers and will quickly retreat to water bodies when faced with land-based predators. Their flight response is a survival strategy that enables them to escape from terrestrial threats and find safety in water, where they are better equipped to evade predators.

Social Interactions: Responses to external stimuli also involve social interactions and communication within the group. Vocalizations, body language, and grooming behaviors play a role in conveying information and maintaining group cohesion during times of stress or changes in their environment.

Capybaras' responses to external stimuli reflect their adaptability and social nature. By relying on communication and cooperation, they enhance their chances of survival and navigate the challenges presented by their ever-changing environment.

4.6 Cognitive Studies and Research on Capybara Intelligence

Cognitive studies and research on capybara intelligence have shed light on their problem-solving abilities, learning capacities, and social behaviors. While they are not as extensively studied as some other animal species, the existing research highlights several key aspects of their cognitive capabilities.

In studies involving puzzle-solving tasks, capybaras have demonstrated problem-solving skills by successfully navigating mazes and overcoming challenges to obtain rewards. These experiments indicate their ability to learn from experiences and apply that knowledge to solve novel problems.

Learning tasks in captivity have revealed capybaras' capacity for associative learning, where they form connections between specific behaviors and rewards. They are quick learners and can adapt their behavior based on reinforcement and positive experiences.

Research on capybara communication has explored their vocalizations and body language, revealing a sophisticated system of signals and expressions that contribute to their social interactions. Their communication plays a crucial role in maintaining group cohesion, coordinating activities, and conveying emotional states.

Observations of capybara social behaviors have also provided insights into their emotional intelligence, showing that they display empathy, nurturing behaviors, and responses to the emotions of other group members. Their social bonds and cooperative care systems further emphasize their emotional awareness and the importance of social connections in their lives.

While cognitive studies on capybaras are still relatively limited compared to other animal species, the existing research underscores their intelligence and complex social behaviors. As interest in capybara cognition grows, further studies may reveal even more intriguing aspects of their intelligence and emotional capabilities.

Chapter 5: Capybaras in Human Culture

Capybaras hold a special place in human culture, inspiring stories, art, and symbolism. Their interactions with humans throughout history have shaped their significance in indigenous folklore, artistic representations, and cultural symbolism. In this chapter, we will explore the cultural connections between capybaras and humans, examining their role in indigenous folklore, art, literature, and their broader cultural significance.

5.1 Capybaras in Indigenous Folklore

In regions where capybaras are native, they often feature prominently in indigenous folklore and mythology. Indigenous communities have coexisted with capybaras for centuries, and their presence in daily life has led to the development of rich cultural narratives and beliefs surrounding these creatures.

In some indigenous folklore, capybaras are portrayed as wise and resourceful creatures. They are often associated with water, fertility, and abundance, given their preference for aquatic habitats and their ability to reproduce and thrive in large social groups. Stories featuring capybaras may emphasize themes of unity, family bonds, and the importance of cooperation within the community.

In other tales, capybaras may be depicted as tricksters or as guides to the spirit world. These stories reflect the diverse perspectives and interpretations of the animal's behavior and interactions with humans.

The cultural significance of capybaras in indigenous folklore lies in their role as symbols of natural harmony and the interconnectedness of all living beings. They serve as reminders of the importance of respecting and living in harmony with nature, as well as the value of community and cooperation within human societies.

5.2 Capybaras in Art and Literature

Capybaras have inspired artists and writers throughout history, making appearances in various forms of art and literature across different cultures. Their unique appearance, gentle demeanor, and intriguing social behaviors have captured the imagination of creators, leading to their inclusion in paintings, sculptures, poems, and stories.

In art, capybaras have been depicted in various styles, ranging from realistic portrayals in naturalistic landscapes to whimsical and fantastical representations in surreal artworks. They often symbolize tranquility, community, and an appreciation for the beauty of the natural world.

Literary works have also featured capybaras as characters or symbols. In some stories, they may represent innocence and vulnerability, while in others, they embody resilience and adaptability. Capybaras' social nature and family-oriented behaviors have inspired narratives centered around themes of friendship, family bonds, and the importance of social connections.

In modern literature, capybaras have even found their way into children's books, becoming beloved characters that teach young readers valuable lessons about cooperation, empathy, and understanding.

Their portrayal in art and literature contributes to the broader cultural recognition of capybaras as captivating and endearing creatures, fostering a sense of appreciation for their place in the natural world.

5.3 Cultural Significance and Symbolism

Capybaras hold cultural significance and symbolism in various regions, often representing different qualities and values depending on the context. Some of the common cultural associations with capybaras include:

Social Harmony: Capybaras' highly social nature and strong family bonds symbolize the importance of unity and cooperation within communities. They represent the idea that strength and resilience can be found in working together and supporting one another.

Abundance and Fertility: Due to their large group sizes and prolific reproductive abilities, capybaras are sometimes associated with abundance and fertility in some cultural contexts. They may symbolize prosperity and the bountiful gifts of nature.

Tranquility and Serenity: Capybaras' calm and gentle demeanor, especially when seen lounging near water bodies, can evoke feelings of tranquility and serenity. In some cultures, they may be seen as symbols of peace and a balanced way of life.

Interconnectedness of Life: Capybaras' role as ecosystem engineers, shaping their habitats through their behaviors, highlights their connection to the natural world and the delicate balance of ecosystems. This connection symbolizes the interdependence of all living beings on Earth.

Spiritual Guides: In some beliefs, capybaras are seen as spiritual guides or totems, representing qualities that humans should strive to embody. They may symbolize attributes like wisdom, adaptability, or intuition.

Overall, the cultural significance and symbolism of capybaras vary across different regions and cultures, reflecting the diverse perspectives and interpretations of these fascinating animals. Their portrayal in human culture contributes to the broader appreciation and understanding of their place in the natural world and their impact on human societies.

5.4 Domestication and Role as Pets

Capybaras have a unique relationship with humans, and in some regions, they have been domesticated and kept as pets. Their docile nature, gentle demeanor, and social behaviors have made them appealing to some individuals as companion animals. However, domestication and keeping capybaras as pets raise various ethical and practical considerations.

In some areas, particularly in South America, capybaras have been kept as pets by indigenous communities and local residents for centuries. They are often considered part of the family and are valued for their companionship and the role they play in daily life. As communal animals, they can easily integrate into human households and form bonds with their human caregivers.

However, keeping capybaras as pets also poses challenges. These social creatures require ample space, appropriate living conditions, and opportunities for social interactions. Meeting their physical, social, and emotional needs can be demanding and may not be feasible for many potential pet owners.

Moreover, domestication raises concerns about the impact on wild populations. As with any wild animal kept in captivity, there is a risk that the demand for pet capybaras could lead to illegal wildlife trafficking or irresponsible breeding practices.

For these reasons, capybara domestication should be approached with caution and responsible pet ownership. Individuals considering keeping capybaras as pets must carefully research their care requirements and ensure they can provide a suitable and enriching environment for these intelligent and social creatures.

5.5 Capybara Conservation Efforts by Humans

As with many wild animal species, capybaras face threats to their natural habitats and populations due to human activities. To counter these threats and preserve capybaras for future generations, various conservation efforts have been initiated by humans.

One of the primary conservation strategies is the protection and preservation of capybara habitats. This involves the establishment of protected areas, such as national parks and reserves, where capybaras and other wildlife can thrive without disturbance from human activities such as deforestation or urban development.

Educational programs also play a vital role in capybara conservation. By raising awareness about the ecological importance of capybaras and their role in maintaining ecosystem balance, conservationists can garner public support and encourage people to take actions that benefit these creatures and their habitats.

Furthermore, research on capybara ecology and behavior is crucial for developing effective conservation plans. Understanding their habitat requirements, migratory patterns, and social dynamics helps conservationists identify priority areas for protection and implement management strategies that support capybara populations.

International cooperation is also essential for capybara conservation, as these animals often inhabit regions that span multiple countries. Collaboration among different nations allows for the establishment of transboundary conservation efforts and the implementation of coordinated conservation plans.

Conservation efforts by humans play a critical role in ensuring the survival and well-being of capybaras and the maintenance of healthy ecosystems where they play a significant role.

5.6 Human Interaction and Encounters with Capybaras

Capybaras' interactions with humans extend beyond domestication and conservation efforts. In regions where they coexist with human populations, capybaras often encounter humans in various settings, including urban areas, agricultural landscapes, and tourist destinations.

In some regions, capybaras have adapted to human-modified landscapes, such as agricultural fields and urban parks. They may graze on crops, leading to conflicts with farmers seeking to protect their livelihoods. Balancing the needs of human communities with capybara conservation is an ongoing challenge in such areas.

Capybaras have also become attractions for ecotourism in some regions, drawing tourists who want to observe these unique creatures in their natural habitats. Responsible ecotourism can provide economic benefits to local communities while promoting capybara conservation and raising awareness about their importance in the ecosystem.

However, interactions with humans can also pose risks to capybaras. Some people may attempt to approach or feed wild capybaras, leading to habituation and potential disruptions to their natural behaviors. Feeding wild capybaras can also expose them to unhealthy diets and create dependency on human-provided food sources.

Human encounters with capybaras should prioritize respect for their natural behaviors and the conservation guidelines in place for their protection. Observing these animals from a safe distance, without attempting to approach or feed them, ensures minimal disturbance to their daily activities.

Chapter 6: Capybara Communication

Capybaras, as highly social animals, rely on a sophisticated system of communication to convey information, express emotions, and maintain social cohesion within their groups. In this chapter, we will explore the various modes of capybara communication, including their vocalizations and sounds, body language and postures, and the importance of scent markings and chemical communication.

6.1 Vocalizations and Sounds

Capybaras are vocal animals, capable of producing a range of vocalizations and sounds to communicate with each other. While their vocal repertoire may not be as diverse as some other animals, their sounds play a crucial role in conveying information within their social groups.

One of the most common vocalizations of capybaras is the purr, which is a soft and rhythmic sound often associated with contentment and relaxation. Purring is typically heard when capybaras are resting or engaging in grooming behaviors, indicating a state of comfort and well-being.

Another important vocalization is the bark, which serves as an alarm call to alert the group to potential dangers or threats. The bark is a high-pitched and sharp sound that is produced when capybaras perceive a predator or any situation that might require the group's attention and response.

Capybaras also emit whining and whistling sounds, which can convey various emotions and intentions. Whining may be used as a form of communication between group members, while whistling sounds are associated with certain social interactions or expressions of emotions.

The vocalizations of capybaras are essential for coordinating activities, alerting each other to potential threats, and expressing emotions within the group. By understanding and responding to their vocal cues, capybaras can maintain social harmony and navigate their environment more effectively.

6.2 Body Language and Postures

In addition to vocalizations, capybaras communicate through various body language and postures, which provide important visual cues to other group members. Their body language conveys emotions, social status, and intentions, contributing to their complex social dynamics and interactions.

Raising the head and standing upright can be a sign of alertness and vigilance. Capybaras often adopt this posture when they sense potential dangers or when they want to maintain a watchful eye on their surroundings.

On the other hand, lowering the head is a submissive gesture, indicating that the individual acknowledges the dominance of another group member. Submissive behaviors are essential for maintaining social order and minimizing conflicts within the group.

Physical contact is also crucial in capybara communication. Grooming behaviors, where individuals clean and groom each other's fur, foster social bonds and reinforce the sense of community within the group. Grooming is especially prevalent among family members and contributes to the cooperative care system observed in capybara herds.

Playful behaviors, such as chasing, wrestling, and running, also play a role in capybara communication. Play is a form of social bonding and serves as a means for young capybaras to practice essential skills in a safe and non-threatening environment.

By paying attention to the body language and postures of their group members, capybaras can interpret the emotional states and intentions of others, contributing to the smooth functioning of their social structure.

6.3 Scent Markings and Chemical Communication

Scent plays a significant role in capybara communication, and they have specialized scent glands that they use to leave scent markings on various objects and vegetation. These scent markings serve as important chemical signals that convey information about individual identity, social status, reproductive status, and territorial boundaries.

CHAPTER 6: CAPYBARA COMMUNICATION

Capybaras have scent glands located near their eyes and on their backs. When they rub these glands on objects or vegetation, they leave behind their distinct scent, which acts as a form of chemical communication.

Scent markings are particularly important in defining and maintaining social hierarchies within capybara groups. Dominant individuals may mark their territory more frequently, reinforcing their status and signaling their presence to others.

In the context of reproductive behaviors, scent markings play a role in attracting potential mates and indicating the reproductive readiness of females. Scent cues can convey information about a female's estrus cycle and reproductive condition, influencing the behaviors and interactions of male group members.

Scent markings also help reduce potential conflicts within the group. By leaving their distinct scent on communal resources, capybaras can signal ownership and establish territorial boundaries. This reduces the need for direct confrontations over resources and minimizes aggression within the group.

Furthermore, scent markings facilitate communication between individuals who may not be in close physical proximity. Capybaras can gather information about the presence and identity of other group members simply by detecting their scent markings on various objects in their environment.

6.4 Social Signals and Gestures

Capybaras are highly social animals, and their interactions within their groups are facilitated by an array of social signals and gestures. These non-vocal forms of communication are essential for maintaining social cohesion, resolving conflicts, and expressing various emotions. By understanding and responding to these social signals and gestures, capybaras can navigate their complex social structures more effectively.

One prominent social signal among capybaras is the head bobbing behavior. Head bobbing is a common gesture used during social interactions, and it can have different meanings depending on the context. For example, during grooming sessions, head bobbing can be a signal of relaxation and contentment. However, in competitive situations, head bobbing can serve as a warning signal or a display of dominance, indicating a desire for the other individual to back off.

Another important social signal is the scent inspection behavior. Capybaras engage in scent inspections by sniffing each other's anogenital region. This behavior allows them to gather essential information about the reproductive status and social rank of other group members. Scent inspections play a significant role in establishing and maintaining social hierarchies within the group.

Social grooming is another crucial aspect of capybara communication. Grooming behaviors involve cleaning and grooming each other's fur, and they serve as a means of bonding and social cohesion within the group. Social grooming reinforces social bonds and reduces tensions, promoting a sense of community among group members.

Tail wagging is yet another social signal in capybaras. A rapidly wagging tail is often a sign of excitement or agitation, while a slow and deliberate tail wag can indicate a relaxed and content state. This gesture helps convey emotional states and intentions during social interactions.

Through these social signals and gestures, capybaras can navigate their intricate social dynamics, establish hierarchies, and foster a sense of unity within their groups.

6.5 Vocal and Non-Vocal Warning Calls

Capybaras use a combination of vocal and non-vocal warning calls to alert their group members of potential dangers and threats in their environment. These warning calls are crucial for the survival of the group, as they enable quick responses to imminent risks and enhance the group's collective vigilance.

One of the most distinctive warning calls of capybaras is the high-pitched bark. When capybaras sense the presence of predators or other potential dangers, they emit sharp and rapid barking sounds. The bark serves as an alarm signal, alerting other group members to the potential threat and prompting them to take evasive actions.

Apart from vocal warning calls, capybaras also use body language to communicate potential dangers. When capybaras detect a threat, they often stand upright and raise their heads to observe their surroundings. This posture signals a state of alertness and readiness to respond to the perceived danger.

In addition to raising their heads, capybaras may also use visual scanning to monitor their surroundings for potential threats. They may turn their heads from side to side, visually inspecting their environment and assessing the presence of predators or other hazards.

The combination of vocal and non-vocal warning calls allows capybaras to effectively communicate and coordinate their responses to threats. By heeding these warning signals, the group can take swift and coordinated actions to ensure their safety and survival.

6.6 Communication in Different Contexts

Capybaras employ different modes of communication in various contexts, adapting their signals and behaviors to suit different social interactions and situations. Whether it is during feeding, grooming, mating, or avoiding potential dangers, their communication strategies vary based on the specific context.

During feeding, capybaras use vocalizations and body language to coordinate their grazing activities and alert each other to the presence of food sources. Gentle vocalizations and relaxed postures often accompany feeding behaviors, reflecting a state of contentment and cooperation within the group.

In grooming interactions, capybaras engage in gentle vocalizations and rhythmic purring sounds, which signify relaxation and bonding. Mutual grooming strengthens social bonds and fosters a sense of trust and companionship among group members.

During mating rituals, capybaras may use a combination of vocalizations, body language, and scent marking to communicate reproductive intentions and receptivity. Scent markings play a crucial role in signaling reproductive readiness and attracting potential mates.

In situations where conflicts arise, capybaras rely on a combination of submissive behaviors, vocalizations, and body postures to defuse tensions and avoid escalating confrontations into aggression. Submissive head bobbing and lowering of the head are common gestures used to express deference and avoid direct confrontations with dominant group members.

Communication in different contexts allows capybaras to adapt their behaviors and signals to effectively navigate their social interactions, respond to changing environments, and ensure the smooth functioning of their social structures.

Chapter 7: Capybaras and their Predators

Capybaras, despite their large size and social nature, are not without their share of predators in the wild. Their natural predators are a significant factor shaping their behavior, group dynamics, and survival strategies. In this chapter, we will explore the natural predators of capybaras, their defense mechanisms and anti-predator behavior, as well as the group defense strategies that capybaras employ to mitigate the risks posed by predators.

7.1 Natural Predators in the Wild

In the wild, capybaras face predation from a range of carnivorous predators. The most common natural predators of capybaras include:

Jaguars (Panthera onca): As apex predators in the Amazon rainforest and other South American habitats, jaguars are formidable hunters that can take down large prey, including capybaras.

Pumas (Puma concolor): Also known as cougars or mountain lions, pumas are stealthy predators that rely on ambush tactics to catch their prey, including capybaras.

Anacondas (Eunectes spp.): Large constrictor snakes like the green anaconda are capable of capturing and suffocating capybaras that come too close to water bodies.

Caimans (Caiman spp.): These crocodilian predators inhabit the waterways where capybaras often seek refuge. Caimans can ambush and attack capybaras when they enter the water.

Harpy Eagles (Harpia harpyja): These powerful raptors are known to prey on young and vulnerable capybaras.

While capybaras have many predators in their natural habitats, they have evolved certain defense mechanisms and strategies to increase their chances of survival.

7.2 Defense Mechanisms and Anti-Predator Behavior

Capybaras exhibit several defense mechanisms and anti-predator behaviors to protect themselves from their natural predators. Some of these strategies include:

Vigilance and Alertness: Capybaras are vigilant animals that remain alert to their surroundings, especially when they are in open areas or near potential hiding spots for predators. Their social structure allows them to have multiple sets of eyes and ears watching for danger, increasing their chances of detecting predators early.

Group Living: Capybaras' preference for living in large social groups provides them with safety in numbers. By sticking together in groups, they can effectively defend against predators and respond collectively to threats.

Speed and Agility: Despite their large size, capybaras are agile and fast runners. When fleeing from predators, they can quickly reach high speeds, making it challenging for predators to catch them.

Diverse Habitat Use: Capybaras often utilize diverse habitats, including dense vegetation and water bodies, to evade predators. They rely on their semi-aquatic nature to find refuge in water when pursued by predators on land.

Alarm Calls: When a capybara detects a potential threat, it emits loud barking sounds to alert other group members. This vocal alarm signal prompts the group to take evasive actions and seek safety.

7.3 Group Defense Strategies

Group defense is a vital aspect of capybara survival. Living in large social groups not only provides capybaras with companionship and cooperation but also strengthens their ability to defend against predators.

When a predator is spotted, capybaras in the group will often gather together and assume a defensive posture. They may stand close to each other, forming a protective barrier around the young and vulnerable members of the group. The collective presence and coordinated movements of the group

CHAPTER 7: CAPYBARAS AND THEIR PREDATORS

can deter some predators from attacking, as the risk of injury outweighs the potential reward of a successful hunt.

Group defense is especially critical during vulnerable times, such as when capybaras give birth to their offspring. Females typically give birth in the water to reduce the risk of predation, and other group members provide additional protection during this period.

The social hierarchy within the group also plays a role in defense strategies. Dominant individuals may take the lead in confronting predators or assessing potential risks. Subordinate group members may follow the lead of dominant individuals to coordinate their responses to threats effectively.

While group defense is a potent strategy, it is not foolproof. Some predators, such as jaguars and anacondas, are formidable hunters with specialized hunting skills that can overcome even the most cohesive group defenses. In such cases, the group's vigilance and agility become essential factors in their survival.

7.4 Predation Impact on Capybara Populations

Predation plays a significant role in shaping capybara populations and their dynamics in the wild. Natural predators exert pressure on capybara populations by influencing their behavior, distribution, and overall survival rates. The impact of predation on capybaras can have both direct and indirect effects on their population size and structure.

Direct predation events, such as successful hunts by predators like jaguars, pumas, anacondas, and caimans, can lead to the loss of individual capybaras. Young, old, or sick individuals are often more vulnerable to predation, as they may have reduced mobility or be less vigilant compared to healthy adults.

Indirectly, predation can affect capybara behavior and distribution patterns. Fear of predators can influence where capybaras choose to forage, rest, or give birth. Areas with higher predation risk may be avoided, leading to changes in habitat use and population density. For instance, capybaras may prefer to stay closer to water, where they can quickly seek refuge from terrestrial predators.

Predation can also influence capybara reproductive success. If predation pressure is high, female capybaras may delay or avoid giving birth during periods of increased risk, which could impact population growth rates. Additionally, the loss of adult capybaras due to predation can disrupt social structures within groups, affecting breeding opportunities and cooperative care for young.

However, it is essential to note that predation is a natural ecological process that helps maintain balance in ecosystems. Predators regulate prey populations, preventing overpopulation that could lead to resource depletion and negative consequences for other species within the ecosystem. Thus, despite the challenges predation poses to capybaras, it is a critical factor in their ecological interactions and coexistence with other species.

7.5 Predator-Prey Relationships and Coexistence

Predator-prey relationships are complex and dynamic interactions that have evolved over millennia. In the case of capybaras and their predators, these relationships are integral to the functioning of their ecosystems. Predators exert selective pressure on capybaras, favoring individuals with certain behavioral traits or adaptations that enhance their chances of survival.

As social animals, capybaras' group living and vigilant behavior are likely adaptations that have evolved in response to predation pressure. Living in large social groups provides capybaras with increased awareness of potential threats and enhances their collective ability to detect predators early. The vocal alarm calls emitted by capybaras serve as an alert system that warns the group of impending danger and enables them to respond collectively.

In turn, capybaras' behaviors and adaptations also influence the behavior of their predators. For example, the presence of a vigilant and cohesive capybara group may deter some predators from initiating a hunt, as the risk of injury or failure may outweigh the potential reward. This dynamic interplay between predator and prey shapes their coexistence and influences population dynamics on both sides.

Predator-prey relationships are an essential aspect of maintaining ecosystem balance. When predators regulate capybara populations, it can prevent overgrazing of vegetation and ensure the ecological integrity of the habitat. Conversely, capybara populations provide a valuable food source for predators, supporting their survival and contributing to the stability of the predator population.

7.6 Human Interventions and Conservation Measures

Human interventions and conservation measures can influence the predator-prey dynamics of capybaras and their predators. In some regions, human activities, such as deforestation, habitat fragmentation, and hunting, can disrupt natural predator-prey relationships and threaten the survival of capybara populations.

Conservation efforts aimed at protecting capybaras and their habitats can indirectly benefit their predator species as well. Establishing protected areas and wildlife corridors helps preserve capybara populations and ensures the availability of suitable habitats for their predators.

Conservation organizations may also implement measures to reduce human-wildlife conflicts, especially in areas where capybaras come into close proximity with human settlements. Educating local communities about the importance of coexisting with capybaras and their predators can help foster positive attitudes towards these animals and encourage tolerance and responsible behavior.

Human intervention can also have negative impacts on capybara populations. For example, illegal hunting or habitat destruction can lead to reduced prey availability for predators, disrupting the balance of predator-prey relationships.

Conservation measures should be carefully designed to consider the broader ecological context and the interactions between capybaras and their predators. A holistic approach that takes into account the needs of both prey and predator species is essential for promoting sustainable coexistence and maintaining healthy ecosystems.

Chapter 8: Capybaras and Human Agriculture

8.1 Crop Damage and Human-Wildlife Conflict

Capybaras are herbivorous animals that primarily feed on vegetation, including grasses, aquatic plants, and agricultural crops. As their natural habitats shrink due to human activities such as deforestation and urbanization, capybaras are increasingly coming into contact with agricultural lands. This interaction can lead to crop damage and human-wildlife conflict, as capybaras seek food resources in cultivated fields.

Crop damage by capybaras can have significant economic implications for farmers. Large groups of capybaras can consume substantial amounts of crops, leading to reduced yields and financial losses for agricultural producers. This crop depredation can be particularly problematic during times of food scarcity, as capybaras may resort to raiding crops to fulfill their dietary needs.

Human-wildlife conflict arises when farmers perceive capybaras as pests that threaten their livelihoods. In response to crop damage, some farmers resort to lethal control methods, such as hunting or poisoning, to reduce capybara populations and protect their crops. However, such measures are often ineffective and can have unintended consequences, including the harm to non-target species and ecosystem imbalances.

8.2 Capybara Impact on Agricultural Lands

The impact of capybaras on agricultural lands varies depending on factors such as habitat availability, capybara population density, and the types of crops cultivated. In regions with abundant natural habitats, capybaras may have less need to venture into agricultural lands. However, as natural habitats diminish, capybaras may increasingly seek food resources in cultivated areas, intensifying the potential for human-wildlife conflict.

Capybaras prefer to forage near water sources, making rice paddies, sugarcane fields, and other crops grown in wet or lowland areas particularly vulnerable to their presence. Additionally, capybaras are prolific diggers, and their burrows can lead to soil erosion and damage to irrigation systems, further exacerbating their impact on agricultural lands.

The ability of capybaras to thrive in close proximity to human settlements and agricultural areas is a testament to their adaptability. As they increasingly overlap with human activities, finding effective solutions to mitigate their impact on crops becomes imperative for promoting coexistence.

8.3 Solutions and Mitigation Strategies

Addressing human-wildlife conflict between capybaras and agriculture requires a balanced and multifaceted approach that considers the needs of both farmers and capybaras. Implementing effective solutions and mitigation strategies can reduce crop damage and promote harmonious coexistence:

Habitat Protection and Restoration: Preserving natural habitats and creating wildlife corridors can help reduce the encroachment of capybaras into agricultural lands. By providing sufficient natural food resources, capybaras are less likely to seek crops as an alternative.

Crop Diversification: Encouraging farmers to diversify their crops can minimize the attractiveness of agricultural lands to capybaras. Planting crops that are less palatable to capybaras or incorporating natural deterrents may reduce crop depredation.

Fencing and Barriers: Installing physical barriers, such as fences, can prevent capybaras from accessing cultivated fields. Electric fencing and other deterrents can also be effective in keeping capybaras away from crops.

Non-Lethal Deterrents: Implementing non-lethal deterrents, such as noise-making devices, scarecrows, or chemical repellents, can discourage capybaras from foraging in agricultural areas without harming them.

Education and Awareness: Raising awareness among farmers about the ecological importance of capybaras and the potential benefits of coexistence can foster more tolerant attitudes towards these animals.

Compensation and Insurance: Providing compensation or insurance to farmers for crop damage caused by wildlife can reduce the economic burden and discourage the use of lethal control methods.

Community-Based Conservation: Involving local communities in conservation efforts and decision-making can foster a sense of ownership and responsibility towards capybara conservation.

Scientific Research: Conducting research on capybara behavior and movement patterns can provide valuable insights for designing effective mitigation strategies and improving our understanding of their interactions with agricultural lands.

By combining these strategies and adopting a collaborative and adaptive approach, it is possible to reduce crop damage and human-wildlife conflict while ensuring the conservation of capybaras and their habitats. Ultimately, achieving coexistence between capybaras and human agriculture is vital for the long-term survival of these charismatic and ecologically important animals.

8.4 Eco-Friendly Farming Practices

In the face of human-wildlife conflict and the impact of capybaras on agricultural lands, adopting eco-friendly farming practices can be a sustainable solution that benefits both farmers and capybaras. Eco-friendly farming practices aim to minimize environmental impact while promoting agricultural productivity. By incorporating practices that are less attractive to capybaras and other wildlife, farmers can reduce crop damage and foster coexistence.

Agroforestry: Integrating trees and shrubs into agricultural landscapes can create diverse habitats and buffer zones that deter capybaras from venturing into crop fields. The presence of natural vegetation can also provide alternative food sources, reducing the reliance on cultivated crops.

Integrated Pest Management (IPM): IPM techniques prioritize biological and cultural methods to manage pests, including capybaras, while minimizing the use of chemical pesticides. Encouraging natural predators of capybaras, such as birds of prey and carnivores, can help control their populations.

CHAPTER 8: CAPYBARAS AND HUMAN AGRICULTURE

Crop Rotation: Crop rotation practices involve planting different crops in a specific sequence to improve soil health and reduce pest pressure. By varying crops, farmers can potentially deter capybaras, as they may be less attracted to certain crops.

Use of Natural Deterrents: Employing natural deterrents, such as companion planting or decoy crops, can discourage capybaras from foraging in cultivated fields. Some plants emit odors or substances that repel capybaras and other herbivores.

Sustainable Water Management: Implementing sustainable water management practices can reduce the attractiveness of agricultural lands to capybaras. Ensuring a steady water supply in natural habitats can discourage capybaras from seeking water sources near crops.

Soil Conservation Techniques: Reducing soil erosion through practices like contour farming and cover cropping can help mitigate damage caused by capybara burrows and preserve the integrity of agricultural lands.

Preservation of Riparian Zones: Protecting riparian zones along water bodies can serve as buffer areas, minimizing the intrusion of capybaras into crop fields.

By adopting these eco-friendly farming practices, farmers can reduce their ecological footprint and create agricultural landscapes that are less conducive to capybara foraging, thereby promoting coexistence and sustainable agriculture.

8.5 Coexistence and Community Involvement

Promoting coexistence between capybaras and human agriculture requires the active involvement of local communities and stakeholders. Engaging with communities and raising awareness about the importance of capybara conservation and ecological balance can foster positive attitudes and behaviors towards these animals.

Education Programs: Developing educational programs that highlight the ecological role of capybaras and the benefits of coexistence can help dispel misconceptions and foster a greater appreciation for these creatures.

Capacity Building: Providing training and resources to farmers on wildlife-friendly practices and non-lethal deterrents can empower them to effectively manage potential conflicts with capybaras.

Community Monitoring: Involving local communities in monitoring capybara populations and their movements can contribute valuable data for scientific research and conservation efforts.

Local Governance: Engaging with local authorities and stakeholders in decision-making processes related to land use and conservation can ensure that capybara habitats are adequately protected.

Eco-tourism and Sustainable Livelihoods: Leveraging the presence of capybaras for eco-tourism activities can generate economic incentives for their conservation, creating sustainable livelihoods for local communities.

Cultural Significance: Recognizing the cultural significance of capybaras in local traditions and folklore can enhance community pride and support for their conservation.

By involving communities in capybara conservation efforts and promoting coexistence, we can foster a sense of shared responsibility for the protection of these creatures and their habitats.

8.6 Economic Benefits of Capybara Conservation

Beyond ecological considerations, capybara conservation can bring about significant economic benefits for local communities and society as a whole:

Eco-Tourism Revenue: Capybaras are charismatic and attract tourists interested in observing wildlife in its natural habitat. Eco-tourism centered around capybara conservation can generate revenue for local communities through wildlife tours and accommodation services.

Biodiversity Conservation: Capybaras are a keystone species in their ecosystems, influencing vegetation dynamics and supporting a wide range of other species. Preserving capybara populations contributes to overall biodiversity conservation and ecosystem health.

Water Resource Management: Capybaras play a role in shaping wetland habitats, which act as vital water reservoirs and contribute to flood regulation. Healthy capybara populations can indirectly benefit water resource management and human settlements.

Scientific Research and Education: Studying capybaras and their interactions with their environment can provide valuable insights into ecological

CHAPTER 8: CAPYBARAS AND HUMAN AGRICULTURE

processes and serve as an educational resource for students and researchers.

Sustainable Agriculture: Encouraging coexistence and implementing eco-friendly farming practices can foster sustainable agricultural systems that preserve natural resources and minimize environmental impacts.

Cultural and Recreational Value: Capybaras hold cultural significance in many regions and are a source of recreational enjoyment for people who appreciate wildlife observation and nature-based activities.

By recognizing and harnessing these economic benefits, society can invest in capybara conservation as a means of ensuring long-term ecological stability and sustainable development.

Chapter 9: Capybaras in Captivity

9.1 Zoos and Conservation Breeding Programs

Capybaras are fascinating and social animals that have become popular attractions in zoos and wildlife parks worldwide. Keeping capybaras in captivity serves multiple purposes, including educational opportunities for the public, research and conservation efforts, and the potential for breeding programs to support species preservation.

Zoos play a crucial role in educating the public about capybaras and their natural behaviors. Visitors have the chance to observe these unique creatures up close, learn about their ecology and social dynamics, and gain an appreciation for their conservation needs. These educational experiences can foster empathy and support for wildlife conservation.

Conservation breeding programs in captivity are undertaken with the goal of maintaining genetically diverse and healthy populations of capybaras. In cases where capybara populations in the wild are threatened or declining, captive breeding can act as a safety net to prevent extinction. If needed, individuals from captive populations can be reintroduced into the wild to bolster wild populations or establish new ones.

To ensure the success and ethical standards of captive breeding programs, it is essential to consider factors such as genetic diversity, animal welfare, and the suitability of release candidates for potential reintroduction. Such programs must adhere to international guidelines and best practices for responsible and sustainable breeding efforts.

9.2 Ethical Considerations in Captive Settings

Keeping capybaras in captivity raises several ethical considerations that must be carefully addressed to ensure the well-being of the animals. Ethical concerns may include animal welfare, enclosure design, social dynamics, and breeding practices.

Animal Welfare: The primary ethical concern in captivity is the welfare of individual capybaras. Zoos and captive facilities must provide appropriate enclosures that meet the physical, social, and behavioral needs of these animals. Enrichment activities, access to water and natural vegetation, and opportunities for social interactions are essential for maintaining the mental and physical health of capybaras in captivity.

Enclosure Design: Captive environments must mimic natural habitats as closely as possible, providing ample space for capybaras to roam, graze, and engage in natural behaviors. Enclosures should also offer shelter and protection from extreme weather conditions to ensure the animals' well-being.

Social Dynamics: Capybaras are highly social animals, and keeping them in isolation can lead to psychological stress and behavioral problems. In captivity, efforts should be made to house capybaras in groups, replicating their natural social structures and promoting positive interactions.

Breeding Practices: Conservation breeding programs should prioritize genetic diversity and avoid inbreeding. Responsible breeding practices involve carefully managing breeding pairs and ensuring that the offspring have the potential for successful reintroduction or contribute to the genetic diversity of the captive population.

Transparency and Education: Zoos and captive facilities should be transparent about their breeding and conservation efforts, as well as their commitment to animal welfare. Education and public outreach can help visitors understand the ethical considerations and conservation goals of captive settings.

By prioritizing the ethical treatment of capybaras in captivity, we can enhance the role of captive facilities as educational centers and conservation partners.

9.3 Behavioral Studies in Captive Capybaras

Captive settings offer unique opportunities for behavioral studies and research on capybaras. Observing capybaras in controlled environments allows researchers to study various aspects of their behavior, social interactions, and responses to environmental stimuli.

Social Behavior: Capybaras' complex social structures can be closely studied in captive groups. Researchers can observe their hierarchy, grooming interactions, and communication patterns, shedding light on their social dynamics and group cohesion.

Reproductive Behavior: Studying capybara reproductive behavior in captivity can provide insights into their mating strategies, courtship rituals, and parental care. Understanding their reproductive biology is crucial for successful breeding programs and potential reintroductions.

Feeding Habits: Captive environments allow researchers to closely monitor capybaras' feeding habits and dietary preferences. Studying their diet can aid in designing optimal nutrition plans for captive populations and provide insights into their ecological role as herbivores.

Enrichment Studies: Behavioral enrichment activities are essential for the mental stimulation and well-being of captive capybaras. Researchers can assess the effectiveness of different enrichment techniques, such as puzzle feeders or sensory enrichment, to enhance the animals' quality of life.

Response to Environmental Changes: Captive environments provide controlled settings to study how capybaras respond to changes in their surroundings, such as alterations in habitat or the introduction of new group members.

Behavioral studies in captivity contribute valuable knowledge to our understanding of capybaras, supporting their conservation and welfare both in captivity and in the wild. The information gained from captive studies can inform conservation efforts, improve management practices, and enhance our appreciation for these remarkable creatures.

9.4 Enrichment and Mental Stimulation

Enrichment and mental stimulation are vital aspects of caring for capybaras in captivity. Providing an environment that meets their physical and psychological needs is essential for their well-being and overall health.

CHAPTER 9: CAPYBARAS IN CAPTIVITY

Enrichment activities aim to stimulate natural behaviors, encourage problem-solving, and alleviate boredom in captive capybaras.

Environmental Enrichment: Environmental enrichment involves creating a dynamic and stimulating living space for capybaras. This can include adding various structures, such as logs, rocks, and hiding spots, to replicate natural habitats. Changing the environment regularly keeps capybaras engaged and encourages exploration.

Feeding Enrichment: Introducing novel feeding methods, such as puzzle feeders or foraging opportunities, can mimic the challenges capybaras face in the wild while searching for food. This type of enrichment encourages natural feeding behaviors and prevents overeating.

Sensory Enrichment: Sensory enrichment engages capybaras' senses by introducing different scents, sounds, and visual stimuli. Scented objects or audio recordings of natural sounds can provide sensory variety, keeping capybaras alert and curious.

Social Enrichment: Capybaras are highly social animals, and social interactions are crucial for their mental well-being. Ensuring they have opportunities to interact with conspecifics through play and grooming is essential for their emotional health.

Training and Positive Reinforcement: Training capybaras using positive reinforcement techniques can foster cooperation and provide mental stimulation. Training sessions also serve as a form of enrichment and enhance the bond between keepers and capybaras.

By prioritizing enrichment and mental stimulation in captivity, we can promote the natural behaviors of capybaras and enhance their overall welfare.

9.5 Challenges of Captive Breeding

Captive breeding programs are essential for the conservation of endangered or threatened species like the capybara. However, they come with their unique set of challenges that must be addressed to ensure the success of these programs:

Genetic Diversity: Maintaining genetic diversity is critical in preventing inbreeding depression and maintaining healthy captive populations. Careful management of breeding pairs and genetic assessments are necessary to avoid genetic bottlenecks.

Reproductive Success: Ensuring successful breeding in captivity can be challenging due to various factors, including compatibility issues between individuals, reproductive health problems, and stress-related factors.

Parental Care: Providing appropriate parental care for offspring born in captivity is crucial for their survival and development. In some cases, parental inexperience or rejection may necessitate human intervention to raise the young.

Behavioral Adaptation: Captive-bred capybaras may face challenges when reintroduced to the wild, as they may not have acquired essential survival skills or behavioral adaptations that their wild counterparts possess.

Space and Resources: Maintaining captive capybaras requires adequate space, resources, and specialized care. These demands can be challenging for some facilities, especially those with limited resources.

Addressing these challenges requires collaboration between zoos, conservation organizations, and researchers. By sharing knowledge and experience, we can continuously improve captive breeding programs and enhance their effectiveness in supporting capybara conservation.

9.6 Reintroduction Efforts and Post-Release Monitoring

Reintroduction efforts play a crucial role in restoring capybara populations in their native habitats. Reintroducing captive-bred individuals to the wild is a complex process that requires careful planning and monitoring to ensure successful acclimatization.

Pre-Release Training: Prior to reintroduction, captive-bred capybaras may undergo pre-release training to develop skills necessary for survival in the wild. This training can include foraging practice, predator avoidance, and acclimatization to natural conditions.

Soft Release: Soft release techniques involve gradually acclimatizing capybaras to their new environment before fully releasing them. This approach helps ease the transition and increases the likelihood of successful adaptation to the wild.

Post-Release Monitoring: Monitoring capybaras after their release is essential for assessing their survival and adaptation to the wild. Tracking their movements, feeding behaviors, and social interactions provides valuable data on their post-release success.

Adaptive Management: Reintroduction efforts should be dynamic and flexible, allowing for adaptive management based on post-release monitoring data. If challenges arise, adjustments to reintroduction strategies can be made to improve outcomes.

Community Involvement: Involving local communities in reintroduction efforts is essential for promoting acceptance and support for the presence of capybaras in their natural habitats.

Reintroduction is a challenging and resource-intensive process, but it is essential for the long-term conservation of capybaras. Successful reintroduction efforts contribute to the restoration of ecosystem balance and the preservation of capybaras as a keystone species in their native habitats.

Chapter 10: Future of Capybaras

10.1 Climate Change and Capybara Habitats

Climate change poses significant challenges for capybaras and their habitats. As temperatures rise and weather patterns become more unpredictable, the distribution and availability of suitable habitats for capybaras may be affected. Changes in precipitation and water availability could impact the wetlands and water bodies on which capybaras depend for food and shelter.

In regions with increasing temperatures, capybaras may face heat stress, affecting their behavior and reproductive success. Heat stress can lead to reduced foraging activity, decreased breeding success, and higher vulnerability to diseases. Additionally, extreme weather events, such as floods and droughts, could disrupt capybara populations and their habitats, leading to population declines or local extinctions.

Adapting to climate change will be crucial for capybaras' long-term survival. Conservation efforts should focus on preserving and restoring critical wetland habitats and maintaining connectivity between suitable areas to allow for population movement and gene flow. Climate-resilient land-use planning can also help identify areas less vulnerable to climate change impacts, ensuring capybara populations have a better chance of persisting in the face of environmental challenges.

10.2 Long-Term Population Trends

Monitoring long-term population trends is essential for understanding how capybaras are faring in their natural habitats. Population studies can provide valuable insights into factors affecting capybara populations, including habitat loss, climate change, hunting, and disease.

CHAPTER 10: FUTURE OF CAPYBARAS

While some capybara populations may be stable or increasing in certain regions, others may be declining due to human activities and environmental pressures. Expanding human settlements, agricultural expansion, and infrastructure development can lead to habitat fragmentation, isolating capybara populations and reducing genetic diversity.

Conservation efforts should prioritize protecting large and interconnected habitats to maintain viable capybara populations. Engaging local communities in conservation initiatives and promoting sustainable land-use practices are key to ensuring the long-term survival of capybaras and preserving their ecological role as ecosystem engineers.

10.3 Technological Advances in Capybara Research

Advancements in technology have significantly enhanced our ability to study capybaras and contribute to their conservation. Cutting-edge research tools and techniques are revolutionizing how we understand their behavior, ecology, and interactions with their environment.

GPS Tracking: GPS tracking devices allow researchers to monitor capybara movements in real-time, providing valuable data on their home range, movement patterns, and habitat use. This information is critical for identifying key areas for conservation and understanding how capybaras respond to environmental changes.

Genetic Analysis: Molecular techniques, such as genetic analysis and DNA barcoding, can help assess the genetic diversity and population structure of capybaras. Understanding genetic relationships between populations informs conservation strategies and captive breeding programs.

Remote Sensing: Remote sensing technologies, such as satellite imagery and drones, enable researchers to assess habitat conditions, monitor land-use changes, and identify suitable areas for capybara conservation. Remote sensing data aid in habitat management and protection efforts.

Non-Invasive Monitoring: Non-invasive monitoring techniques, such as camera traps and acoustic recorders, allow researchers to study capybara behavior without direct human interference. These methods provide insights into elusive behaviors and reduce stress on the animals.

Disease Surveillance: Advances in disease surveillance methods contribute to understanding and managing health issues in capybara populations. Early detection of diseases is crucial for implementing targeted conservation measures.

Climate Modeling: Climate models help predict future environmental changes, allowing researchers to assess the potential impact on capybara habitats and develop adaptation strategies.

By leveraging these technological advances, researchers can gain a deeper understanding of capybaras and their ecological roles, inform conservation efforts, and ensure effective management of their populations for the future.

10.4 Collaborative Conservation Initiatives

Effective conservation of capybaras requires collaboration among various stakeholders, including governments, non-governmental organizations (NGOs), local communities, researchers, and zoological institutions. Collaborative conservation initiatives harness the collective knowledge, resources, and expertise of different groups to address challenges and implement comprehensive strategies for capybara protection.

Multi-Stakeholder Partnerships: Collaborative conservation initiatives bring together stakeholders with diverse interests, such as conservationists, scientists, policymakers, and community representatives. These partnerships foster a shared understanding of the issues and promote collective decision-making.

Community Engagement: Involving local communities in conservation initiatives is vital, as they often share spaces with capybaras and are directly affected by conservation efforts. Engaging local people in education, research, and decision-making builds a sense of ownership and stewardship over capybara habitats.

Habitat Protection and Restoration: Collaborative efforts can focus on preserving and restoring critical capybara habitats, including wetlands, riparian zones, and floodplains. Protected areas, wildlife reserves, and land-use planning are essential tools in habitat conservation.

Conservation Education: Raising awareness about the ecological importance of capybaras and the need for their protection is fundamental.

CHAPTER 10: FUTURE OF CAPYBARAS

Educational programs can target schools, local communities, and tourists to foster empathy and support for capybara conservation.

Advocacy and Policy: Collaborative conservation initiatives can advocate for policies that promote capybara protection and sustainable land-use practices. Aligning conservation goals with national and international policy frameworks enhances the legal protection of capybaras and their habitats.

Capacity Building: Building the capacity of local organizations and individuals involved in capybara conservation ensures the long-term sustainability of conservation efforts. Training in research techniques, community engagement, and advocacy empowers stakeholders to be effective agents of change.

10.5 Global Efforts for Capybara Protection

Capybaras are not confined to one region or country; they inhabit several countries across South America. Protecting capybaras requires global collaboration and coordinated efforts among countries where they occur. International initiatives play a critical role in promoting capybara conservation and preserving their habitats.

International Agreements: International treaties and agreements, such as the Convention on Biological Diversity (CBD) and the Ramsar Convention on Wetlands, facilitate collaboration among countries for biodiversity conservation, including capybaras and their habitats.

Research and Data Sharing: Sharing research findings and data among scientists and conservation organizations globally enhances our understanding of capybara populations and informs conservation strategies.

Transboundary Conservation: Capybaras often inhabit regions that cross international borders. Transboundary conservation initiatives facilitate cooperation between neighboring countries to protect capybara populations that move freely across borders.

Sustainable Tourism: Promoting sustainable tourism practices that prioritize capybara welfare and habitat conservation can generate economic incentives for local communities and support conservation efforts.

Fundraising and Support: International organizations and donors can provide financial support for capybara conservation projects in countries where resources are limited.

Global efforts for capybara protection reflect the interconnectedness of wildlife and ecosystems worldwide. By collaborating on a global scale, we can ensure the long-term survival of capybaras and preserve their ecological contributions to the ecosystems they inhabit.

10.6 The Importance of Preserving Nature's Social Giants

Capybaras are nature's social giants, known for their strong family bonds, complex social structures, and cooperative behaviors. Their role as ecosystem engineers and keystone species highlights their significance in shaping and maintaining healthy ecosystems.

Ecosystem Engineering: Capybaras significantly impact their habitats through their feeding and burrowing activities. Their grazing influences vegetation growth and dynamics, while their burrows provide shelter for other species during floods and dry periods.

Biodiversity Support: Capybaras contribute to the overall biodiversity of their ecosystems by supporting the populations of predators and prey, acting as prey for several predators, and serving as hosts for various parasites.

Seed Dispersal: Capybaras aid in seed dispersal by consuming fruits and seeds and then depositing them through their scat. This activity promotes vegetation regeneration and enhances forest diversity.

Social Learning: Their social nature facilitates social learning among capybaras. Young individuals learn vital skills and behaviors from older members of their group, contributing to their adaptability and survival.

Ecotourism and Education: Capybaras are charismatic animals that attract ecotourists and nature enthusiasts. Their presence can generate revenue for local communities through tourism and provide opportunities for education about wildlife conservation.

Indicator Species: Capybaras can serve as indicator species, providing insights into the health and status of their habitats. Monitoring capybara populations can alert researchers to environmental changes and potential threats to other species in the ecosystem.

Preserving nature's social giants like capybaras is not only crucial for their own survival but also for the health and balance of entire ecosystems. By protecting capybaras and their habitats, we safeguard the rich biodiversity of South American wetlands and maintain ecological stability in the regions they inhabit.

Conclusion: Capybaras - Nature's Social Giants

Throughout this comprehensive exploration of capybaras, we have embarked on a captivating journey into the lives of nature's social giants. From their evolutionary origins to their complex social structures, from their ecological significance to their interactions with humans, capybaras have revealed themselves as remarkable creatures deserving of our admiration and conservation efforts.

In Chapter 1, we were introduced to the world of capybaras, discovering their unique characteristics, evolutionary history, and physical adaptations that allow them to thrive in their wetland habitats. Their semi-aquatic lifestyle and herbivorous diet set them apart from other rodents, making them intriguing subjects of study.

Chapter 2 delved into capybara ecology, shedding light on their role as ecosystem engineers. Their grazing and burrowing activities significantly influence their habitats, shaping the landscape and supporting biodiversity. We learned how capybaras play a crucial role in seed dispersal and supporting the populations of predators and prey, showcasing their significance in maintaining ecological balance.

In Chapter 3, we explored the heart of capybara social life. Their complex social structures, family units, and communication systems highlighted their strong social bonds and cooperative behaviors. From playful interactions to conflict resolutions, capybaras showcased the depth of their emotional intelligence and the importance of their social communities.

Chapter 4 revealed the cognitive abilities of capybaras, demonstrating their problem-solving skills, learning capabilities, and even their use of tools. Beyond their social dynamics, capybaras displayed intelligence and adaptability, further establishing them as nature's social and intelligent giants.

In Chapter 5, we discovered the cultural significance of capybaras in indigenous folklore, art, and literature. Revered as symbols of communal living and appearing as characters in myths, capybaras have woven themselves into the fabric of human culture. We also explored their domestication and the efforts made for their conservation in the wild.

Chapter 6 unveiled the various forms of communication capybaras employ, from vocalizations to scent markings. Their intricate communication systems play a pivotal role in maintaining group cohesion and facilitating interactions in their social communities.

Chapter 7 provided insights into capybaras' interactions with predators, showcasing their defense mechanisms and predator-prey relationships. These interactions underscore their essential role in the natural balance of their ecosystems.

Chapter 8 addressed the complex relationship between capybaras and human agriculture. We explored the challenges of crop damage and human-wildlife conflicts while identifying eco-friendly farming practices and coexistence strategies to promote harmonious interactions.

Chapter 9 delved into the world of capybaras in captivity, from zoos and breeding programs to ethical considerations. We learned how enrichment and mental stimulation are crucial for their well-being, and how collaborative conservation initiatives and global efforts are vital for their protection and preservation.

In Chapter 10, we considered the future of capybaras, facing challenges posed by climate change and long-term population trends. We recognized the importance of proactive conservation strategies, technological advances, and collaborative efforts in safeguarding the future of these gentle giants.

In conclusion, capybaras have captivated us with their unique traits, complex social structures, and vital ecological contributions. They hold a significant place in human culture, symbolizing communal living and captivating our imagination in folklore and literature. As we navigate the complexities of their conservation, we must embrace a holistic approach that involves collaborative efforts, sustainable practices, and community engagement.

Capybaras are not just icons of the animal kingdom; they are symbols of the interconnectedness of life on Earth. Their survival is intertwined with the health and balance of their ecosystems, reminding us of the delicate web of life we must cherish and protect. By valuing these nature's social giants and recognizing their significance in the natural world, we can pave the way for a future where capybaras continue to thrive, enriching our lives and the ecosystems they call home. Let us embark on a journey of conservation, appreciation, and admiration for these remarkable creatures, as we join hands in preserving the magic of capybaras - nature's social giants.

Printed in Great Britain
by Amazon